AMAZONIAN SISTERHOOD

Northwater

CONSTANTINE ISSIGHOS

Copyright 2012 © Constantine Issighos. Published in Canada. Printed in U.S.A. No part of this book may be reproduced or transmitted in any form or by any means, electronic or mechanical, including photocopying, recording, and/or by any information storage and retrieval system except by a reviewer who may quote brief passages in a review to be printed in a magazine, newspaper, or on the web without written permission in writing from the author/publisher. For information, please contact www.awaqkunabooks.com

NorthWater is an imprint of Awaqkuna Books Inc.

Vol. 7 of THE AMAZON EXPLORATION SERIES:
AMAZONIAN SISTERHOOD

Library and Archives Canada

ISBN 978-0-9878599-6-9

Library and Archives Canada Cataloguing in Publication

ATTENTION CHILDRENS ASSOCIATIONS, BOOK STORES, PUBLIC OR PRIVATE LIBRARIES: quantity discounts are available on bulk purchases of this book series.

THE AMAZON EXPLORATION SERIES

Children's Books
by
Constantine Issighos

1. Upper Amazon Voyage by River Boat
2. The People of the River
3. The Children of the River
4. Amazon's Nature of Things
5. Echoes of Nature: a Beautiful Wild Habitat
6. The Amazon Rainforest
7. Amazonian Sisterhood
8. Amazon River Wolves
9. Amazonian Landscapes and Sunsets
10. Amazonian Canopy: the Roof of the World's Rainforest
11. Amazonian Tribes: a World of Difference
12. Birds and Butterflies of the Amazon
13. The Great Wonders of the Amazon
14. The Jaguar People
15. The Fresh Water Giants
16. The Call of the Shaman
17. Indigenous Families: Life in Harmony with Nature
18. Amazon in Peril
19. Giant Tarantulas and Centipedes
20. The Amazon Ethno-Botanical Garden
21. The Real Amazon Tribal Warriors

Photographs serve as an important and informative reference for understanding the indigenous sisterhoods of the Amazon River basin of South America. The photographs in this book provide a window into the daily lives of Amazonian women, showing their body panting, crafts and their participation in cultural traditions.

In order to understand the Amazonian Sisterhood and its significance, one must understand the tribal culture and the status of women within it. The women of the Amazon live in many different cultural environments and have adapted their daily lives to the various ecosystems. Within this culture of adaptation and survival, they live without the cultural taboos against girls and women showing their naked breasts or of either sex displaying their naked bodies..

In the last several years, previously uncontacted tribes of the Upper Amazon have received considerable attention in the world's news and popular press. Photos show astonishing scenes of naked women warriors with black and red body painting and facial tattoos, wielding bows and arrows.

Brave women warriors such as the Amazons' of Greek myth have spread through many cultures. The word *Amazon* is used to describe beautiful women in *Amazonomachies,* which was an artform showing battles (machies) between Amazon-women and Greek-male warriors. In the myth, the Amazons were trained to use all weapons and to excel in individual combat. The Amazon women were portrayed as being honourable, brave and represented rebellion against sexism. These mythological tales spread quickly and soon stories of the Amazon women-warriors were portrayed in literature. In the mid-1900, the popular comic books *Wonder Woman* was a female warrior in the Amazonian tradition.

Popular believe states that the Amazon River was named after the female warriors.

According to early legend; written by the explorer Francisco de Orellana in 1542, some of the most violent natives he encounter in the Amazon were women warriors. Women warriors appeared to be in front lines in the confrontation between the explorers and the natives. This legend contributed to the Greek myth-inspired name of the warrior women; and Orellana ultimately named the region, *Amazonas*.

The Amazon myth started by the Greek story-teller and historian Diodorous of Sicily who, in the second century B.C. introduced the story of the women warriors, *Amazonas*.

The ancient Amazon region was located in the coast of North Africa, which was reigned by gynaecocracy; which means that only women were qualified to joint the ruling and warriors' class. This region was ruled by a Queen *Myrina*. Her army consisted of 30,000 female foot soldiers and 3,000 cavalry. The Queen Myrina successfully fought a number of male dominated armies along the coast of Algiers, Libya and Egypt. In a particular battle the Queen Myrina fell and her brave female soldiers scattered.

It became clear to me that a clearing in the middle of the rainforest, near the riverbanks, indicates the presence of a village. This village area is divided up by zones arranged in concentric circles, with the communal house *(maloca)* having a rounded base and a cone-shaped roof, at the center. The communal house has the capacity to provide shelter for about 80 people. It is divided into internal circular sections *(amaca)* where the women cook the communal meals. A space around the amaca is divided into various shelters for extended family use. Surrounding the communal house there is a designated space (*jororo*) used as a meeting place for the women and which can also be used for festivals. There the women scrape *manioc,* cook, sew and work on their crafts.

Near the communal house there are small gardens—one per family—where women cultivate vegetables, tobacco, cotton and medicinal plants. These products are in high demand in the region and form the main trade among villages in the area. The gardens mark the end of the village clearing, always a distance which can be crossed on foot.

Women participate in a whole series of work activities and rituals that organize time and space in the life of the village. Their hand-woven baskets are very fine, reminiscent of Cherokee basketry. They weave intricate geometric designs and animals and use a variety of natural vegetable dyes to create colour and shades. They weave many drawings which are inspired by the animals found in the rainforest.

Their flat serving baskets are the "cosmograms" of their mythological universe. They show the flat hemisphere of the dome of the heavens, and circular fields filled with complex designs represent atmospheric elements and animal symbols associated with various aspects of their environment. In addition, some designs are associated with the respective sexes by their actual form and application--twill-woven decorated baskets are male, carved wicker-woven baskets are female.

The bells shaped baskets—called Wuwas—are also made by the women of the tribe using natural vegetable dyes and they are decorated with wonderfully intricate designs. The shape of the basket follows the general shape of a woman's body. This design was first used in burden baskets which were carved it fit snugly onto a woman's back. Of course, women still weave utilitarian burden baskets, but the bell shaped

Wuwas have evolved into an artistic basket used in the huts as containers while retaining the burden basket shape. Round baskets are also made by women; they are very sturdy, with a symmetrically shaped and are decorated with the likenesses of jungle animals.

Visitors to the Amazon River often see girls and women of all ages bathing and swimming in order to cool off from the extreme heat of the tropical rainforest. Tribal women exhibit meticulous personal hygiene that helps them maintain their health in a harsh environment. They are not "modest" or ashamed of their bodies. Virtually all the tribal women of the Amazon River Basin do not wear any clothes.

Indigenous women are the frontrunners against environmental destruction by big oil, gas and logging companies. In the Ecuadorian, Brazilian and Peruvian rainforest, women organize themselves. Counting on the army and policemen's reluctance to shoot women, they stand up against polluters. Mothers, Sisters and Grandmothers have openly declared to the national leaders that they will not allow their children and youth to become slaves of big oil and gas companies. This is a non-negotiable decision for the Amazonian *Kichwa* women. Unconfirmed reports indicate that the Kichwa women have also told their men to stand up and fight or they should start looking for other women… in another territory.

Indigenous women should be recognized for how important their resistance to big oil and gas companies is for humanity and the planet. They stand up because they know that polluted rivers, polluted air and soil erosion create poverty, human rights violations and will destroy their way of life. Indigenous women suffer more from polluted rivers and oil contamination as it is mostly the women who use water to cook, wash and irrigate their family gardens.

When the soil in their small family-garden plots erodes due to industrial deforestation more of the soil is washed into the tributaries. The water quality is affected. Gradually the tributaries silt up, increasing the likehood of local flooding in the low-lying areas downstream.

The forest provides protection for the village and a vegetative cover over the soil in the family plot. Through the nutrient cycle, vegetation helps to maintain the soil fertility. When it rains, the nutrients enter the soil and plant roots absorb the dissolved nutrients. When the leaves fall, small species, such as worms and insects break down the nutrients. Hence, the fertility of the soil is maintained, and the family garden plot produces enough food for all family members.

While the indigenous men are hunters and gatherers, it is the women who are the land cultivators. However, as a family unit, they rely on the Amazon rainforest for their food, shelter and clothing, thus maintaining their traditional way of life and culture. When pollution affects them, they are forced to move out of the area, and many villagers find it difficult to adapt to a lifestyle outside the Amazonian rainforest.

Collectively, women observe the cultural and ritual traditions which form the shamanic cosmological system in the Amazonian family structure. They are proponents of the shamanic mentality that believes in the existence of the invisible world of the spirits, and in the spirits of the terrestrial world. These systems are interrelated- the Earth is the home of the mortals, where the invisible spirits remain beyond human's visual perception.

In the sky, or more specifically above it, live the good spirits. This category is an extension of themselves as women. The spirits of the terrestrial world materialize in human form but generally remain invisible. The shamanic rituals maintain the world in a fragile balance between the Good Spirits (*Hemoki*) and the Evil Spirits (*Kamari*).

Tonight, the moon shines the way for villagers and visitors alike. Narrow pathways open up before me as I wander through cluster of banana trees. The darkness of the night compliments the moon and inspires me to make wishes full of hope for the future.

The next morning I, as usual, go to take pictures, this time entering the next village uninvited. I see beautiful women and girls sitting on the trunk of a fallen tree and I start taking pictures of them. They are wearing short dresses and they spend time romancing the men. It was awesome. However, as I am taking pictures, my eyes focus on five men, dressed in tradition clothes and carrying long machetes, who are walking towards me. I am able to straighten myself, and I walk towards them, first slowly and then faster. I crossed paths with a young woman who guesses why I am visiting her village. I notice that she seems pale and nervous and--as she hugs me--she invites me to sit by the fallen mango tree. She takes my hand and guides me towards the end of the trunk. Soon the men reached me. Without perceiving any more danger, I pause as if I was running into old acquaintances, and I calmly greet them. I guess I will never know how close I came to being killed.

The Sisterhood of the indigenous women interacts with the legends of the shamanic culture and embraces the many positive values and attributes inspired by their female ancestors. It is open to all women seeking a spiritual connection. It is this spirit of potential growth that unites women to build their independence, self-reliance, character, sisterhood and devotion to female divinity. It is this code of living, honouring the sisters of their village, which makes their lives sacred.

The Amazon Exploration Series   *Constantine Issighos*

AMAZONIAN SISTERHOOD

The Amazon Exploration Series   *Constantine Issighos*

Amazonian Sisterhood   *15*

The Amazon Exploration Series *Constantine Issighos*

Amazonian Sisterhood 19

The Amazon Exploration Series   *Constantine Issighos*

Amazonian Sisterhood   *21*

The Amazon Exploration Series   *Constantine Issighos*

Amazonian Sisterhood   *23*

The Amazon Exploration Series   *Constantine Issighos*

Amazonian Sisterhood   25

The Amazon Exploration Series   *Constantine Issighos*

Amazonian Sisterhood

The Amazon Exploration Series   *Constantine Issighos*

Amazonian Sisterhood

The Amazon Exploration Series   *Constantine Issighos*

Amazonian Sisterhood   *33*

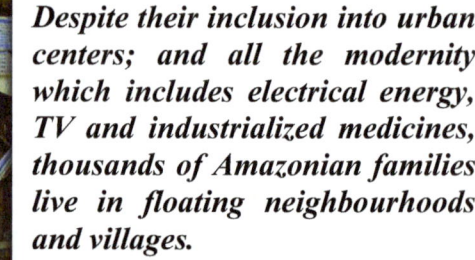

Despite their inclusion into urban centers; and all the modernity which includes electrical energy, TV and industrialized medicines, thousands of Amazonian families live in floating neighbourhoods and villages.

The Amazon Exploration Series   *Constantine Issighos*

Every family owns its own canoe; a much needed necessity, which provides transportation to and from the coastal towns; and a means for children to go to school, families to attend church services and to get medical attention.

Amazonian Sisterhood   35

Floating community structures are an economical way of providing one's family with a much needed shelter, an abundant diet of fish and enough space to raise small domesticated animals such as poultry.

The Amazon Exploration Series   *Constantine Issighos*

Women do casual work as street cleaners, sell fish in the markets or crafts to the tourists.

Amazonian Sisterhood   *37*

Constantine Issighos *The Amazon Exploration Series*

TRIBAL CRAFTS

Amazonian Sisterhood

For visitors to the jungle city of Iquitos, it is quite common to see indigenous women selling their geometrically designed tapestries, ceramics and jewellery.

The Amazon Exploration Series *Constantine Issighos*

The Shapibo tribe are well known for maintaining their strong tribal identity through complex, sophisticated and geometric patterns in their ceramics and basket weaving.

Amazonian Sisterhood

The Amazon Exploration Series   *Constantine Issighos*

The ceramic pieces are extremely soft and light weight and their technique is all done manually without the use of a pottery wheel.

Amazonian Sisterhood

The Amazon Exploration Series *Constantine Issighos*

Amazonian Sisterhood

The women, rather than the men, are the village artists; they are the ones who maintain the tribal artistic tradition, passing it down from mother to daughter.

In the urban open markets, one can see the traditional women's occupations and their dress — a conservative western style far different from their indigenous counterparts.

A visitor can also find the jungle berry Acai (a-sigh-ee) in these open markets. Women collect this berry for its exotic and health benefits. Acai was part of the diet of the Amazon tribes long before the discovery of the Americas.

www.ingramcontent.com/pod-product-compliance
Lightning Source LLC
Chambersburg PA
CBHW041754040426
42446CB00001B/32